Withdrawn

ISRAEL

Marcia Gresko

Lerner Publications Company • Minneapolis

Lerner Publications Company
A division of Lerner Publishing Group, Inc.
241 First Avenue North
Minneapolis, MN 55401 U.S.A.

Website address: www.lernerbooks.com

Library of Congress Cataloging-in-Publication Data

Gresko, Marcia S.
    Israel / by Marcia Gresko.
        p.   cm. —   (Country explorers)
    Includes index.
    ISBN: 978–0–8225–9414–7 (lib. bdg. : alk. paper)
    1. Israel—Juvenile literature. 2. Israel. I. Title.
DS102.95G73 2009
956.94—dc22   2007037101

Manufactured in the United States of America
1 2 3 4 5 6 – PA – 14 13 12 11 10 09

Table of Contents

Welcome!

Let's explore Israel! This country lies in the Middle East. Israel looks like an arrow pointing down.

Israel's northern neighbor is Lebanon. To the east of Israel sit Syria and Jordan. Egypt shares Israel's southwestern border. In the south, Israel meets the Gulf of Aqaba. The Gulf of Aqaba is part of the Red Sea. The Mediterranean Sea lies to the west.

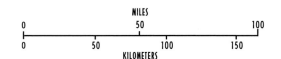

MILES
0   50   100
0   50   100   150
KILOMETERS

Israel's western coast is on the Mediterranean Sea.

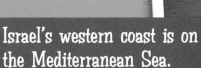

4

N

MEDITERRANEAN
SEA

LEBANON

SYRIA

Israel

MT.
MERON

GOLAN
HEIGHTS

MT.
TABOR

SEA OF
GALILEE

SAMARIAN
HILLS

WEST BANK

JORDAN RIVER

Tel Aviv-Jaffa

Jerusalem ★

ISRAEL

GAZA
STRIP

WEST BANK

DEAD SEA

JUDEAN
HILLS

JORDAN

NEGEV
DESERT

EGYPT

MIDDLE EAST

GULF
OF
AQABA

🏔	mountains
▦	highlands
▦	desert
▦	Great Rift Valley
▦	coastal plains
★	country's capital
-----	disputed border

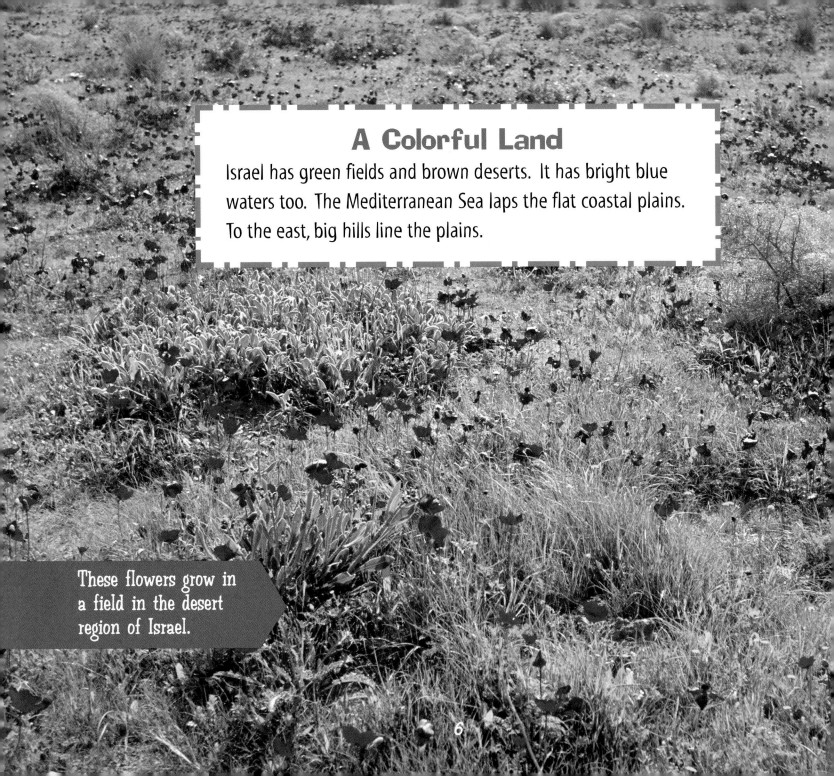

A Colorful Land

Israel has green fields and brown deserts. It has bright blue waters too. The Mediterranean Sea laps the flat coastal plains. To the east, big hills line the plains.

These flowers grow in a field in the desert region of Israel.

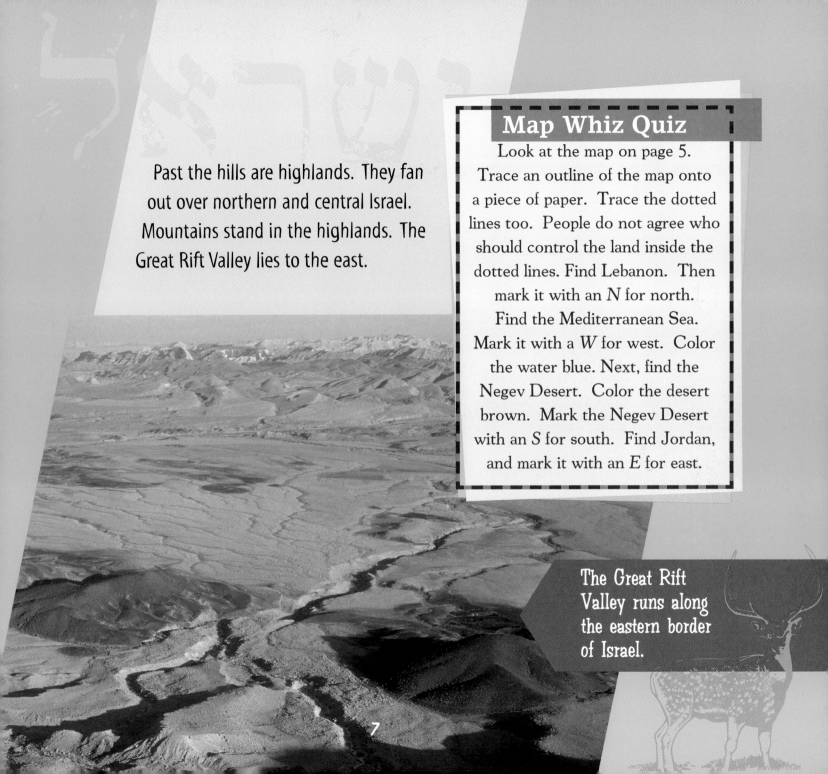

Past the hills are highlands. They fan out over northern and central Israel. Mountains stand in the highlands. The Great Rift Valley lies to the east.

Map Whiz Quiz

Look at the map on page 5. Trace an outline of the map onto a piece of paper. Trace the dotted lines too. People do not agree who should control the land inside the dotted lines. Find Lebanon. Then mark it with an *N* for north. Find the Mediterranean Sea. Mark it with a *W* for west. Color the water blue. Next, find the Negev Desert. Color the desert brown. Mark the Negev Desert with an *S* for south. Find Jordan, and mark it with an *E* for east.

The Great Rift Valley runs along the eastern border of Israel.

Heading South

The Sea of Galilee sits in the Great Rift Valley. The Jordan River flows south from this big sea. The Jordan is Israel's biggest river.

The Jordan River flows from the Sea of Galilee along the eastern border of Israel.

It winds down through the Great Rift Valley. The Jordan empties into the Dead Sea. That sea is the lowest spot on Earth. The water in the Dead Sea is very salty. Fish can't even live in it.

South of the Dead Sea is the Negev Desert. The desert is hot and rocky. It covers the southern half of Israel.

Wild Israel

Hundreds of different kinds of birds and butterflies fly over Israel. Gazelles, wild boars, and jackals roam the hills. Foxes and wildcats live in the wooded areas. In the desert, snakes and lizards sun themselves. Ibex *(below)* scramble up rocky cliffs in the mountains.

The Dead Sea is so salty, people can easily float in it.

Dawn brings a golden glow to buildings in Jerusalem, including the Dome of the Rock *(center)*.

Golden Jerusalem

Jerusalem is the capital of Israel. The city sits on a hilltop in the highlands. People used yellow stone to build most of Jerusalem. It looks as if it were made of gold.

The western half of Jerusalem looks modern. But the eastern half of the city is old. Lively open-air markets pack eastern Jerusalem. And ancient buildings line the streets. Some buildings are a thousand years old!

Dear Aunt,

Shalom! That means hello in Israel. We explored Jerusalem today. We played hide-and-seek on top of the walls of the Old City. Then we splashed through knee-deep water in King Hezekiah's Tunnel. That is an ancient waterway. It cuts through rock under the city. It's deep and dark! I'm sure glad I had my flashlight.
Shalom! (That also means good-bye here.)

Your

You

Anyw

Jerusalem

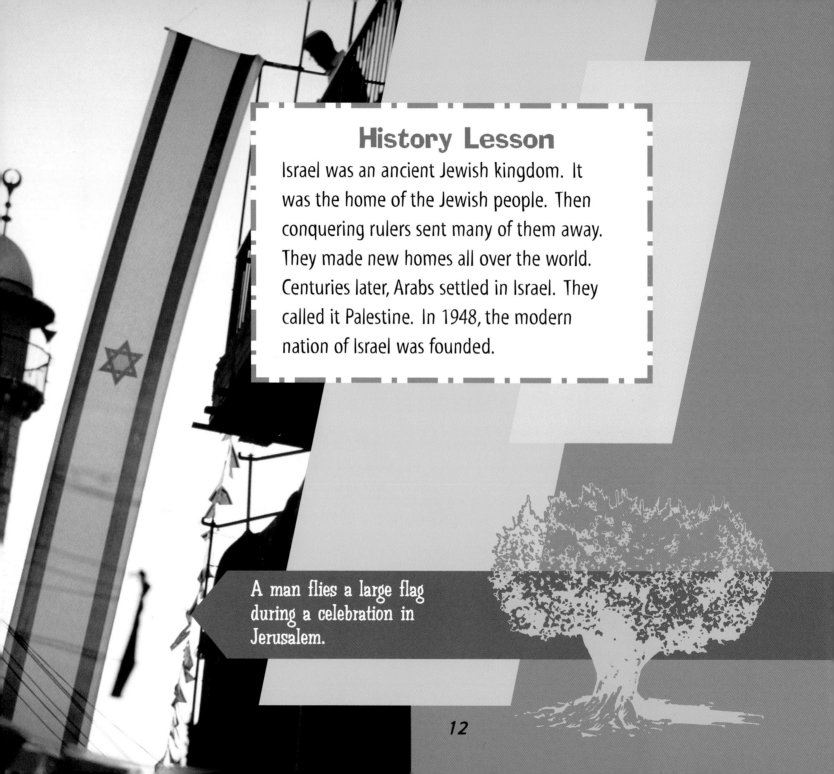

History Lesson

Israel was an ancient Jewish kingdom. It was the home of the Jewish people. Then conquering rulers sent many of them away. They made new homes all over the world. Centuries later, Arabs settled in Israel. They called it Palestine. In 1948, the modern nation of Israel was founded.

A man flies a large flag during a celebration in Jerusalem.

12

Many Jewish people moved to modern Israel. They wanted to live in their original homeland. After a war, many Arabs left. But others stayed. They wanted to control part of Israel. Their people had lived there for more than one thousand years. These days, Jews and Arabs in Israel do not always get along.

The Holocaust

The Holocaust was a terrible event. It happened during World War II (1939–1945). People called Nazis sent millions of Jews to concentration camps. The Nazis treated the Jews badly at these camps. They killed millions of Jews. After the war, many of the Holocaust survivors moved to Israel. Monuments and museums help Israelis remember the Holocaust.

A man visiting the Yad Vashem museum in Jerusalem looks at photos of Jews who died during the Holocaust.

Different Faces

Most Israelis are Jews. But their ancestors came from many different continents. Ancestors are relatives who lived long ago.

Friends and family celebrate a Jewish holiday.

14

Make Yourself at Home!

People who move to Israel might speak French, German, Polish, Hungarian, Ethiopian, or Russian. The Israeli government has set up centers to help newcomers learn how to become part of Israel.

This man wears the clothing of an Orthodox Jew. Orthodox Jews strictly follow Jewish teachings.

The Jewish people of Israel do not look, talk, or dress alike. They eat different foods. They listen to different music. And they speak different languages. These people work together to make Israel a good place to live.

15

The Arabs

About one million Arabs live in Israel. Arabs have lived
in the area since the middle of the 600s C.E. Most Israeli
Arabs are Muslims. Muslims follow the religion of Islam.

Arab schoolchildren
celebrate in Israel.

16

In years past, most Arabs lived on small farms. These days, more Arabs live in cities. Many grown-ups work in shops. Others have construction jobs. Arabs usually speak Arabic.

Nomads

Some Arabs are Bedouin. The Bedouin live in the desert. Some Bedouin are nomads. Nomads move from place to place. But other Bedouin have settled in desert towns. They farm there. And many of their children go to school.

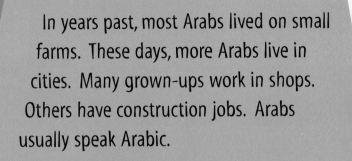

Many Bedouin people use camels in Israel's desert.

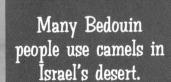

17

City Life

Most Israelis live in cities. Many people live in tall apartment buildings. Some apartments have balconies. Families can relax there on hot nights.

These tall buildings in the Israeli city of Tel Aviv-Jaffa are near the beach.

All in the Family

Here are the Hebrew words for family members.

grandfather	sabba	(SAH-bah)
grandmother	savta	(SAHV-tah)
uncle	dod	(dohd)
aunt	dodda	(DOH-dah)
father	abba	(AH-bah)
mother	eema	(EE-mah)
son	ben	(behn)
daughter	bat	(baht)
brother	ach	(ach)
sister	achot	(ah-CHOT)

Kids spend most days at school. Moms and dads spend their weekdays at work. On weekends, Israelis in the city can go to museums and restaurants. Some drive to the beach or go to a park.

This family enjoys time at the beach in Israel.

On a Kibbutz

Some Israeli kids live on a kibbutz. A kibbutz is a settlement in the country. Each kibbutz is like a village. It has houses, shops, and a school. Farm fields usually lie nearby. And there might be a factory on the kibbutz.

All members of a kibbutz help out with work, even teens and children.

People on a kibbutz eat meals together. They celebrate holidays together. Everyone takes turns doing different jobs. A worker might wash dishes for a few weeks. Then the worker might pick fruit or vegetables.

The Children's House

Kids who live on a kibbutz usually go to a children's house after school. They play and hang out there. The littlest children use them as day care centers.

Kibbutzniks (people who live and work on a kibbutz) eat together.

21

Religion

Judaism is Israel's main religion. It is the oldest religion in the world. Jews believe in one God. Their holy book is called the Torah. The Torah tells about Jewish history. It includes the laws of Judaism. The laws tell Jews how to live good lives.

The Torah is the holy book for Jews. It tells of their history.

This Muslim girl reads from the Quran in a mosque in the West Bank city of Jenin.

Other Israelis are Muslims. Muslims also believe in one God. The name of their God is Allah. Allah's knowledge and understanding is recorded in a sacred book. This book is called the Quran. The Quran is sacred to Muslims.

23

Two Languages

Hebrew and Arabic are Israel's two main languages. Hebrew and Arabic each have their own alphabet. Both languages are written from right to left. That is the opposite direction of written English.

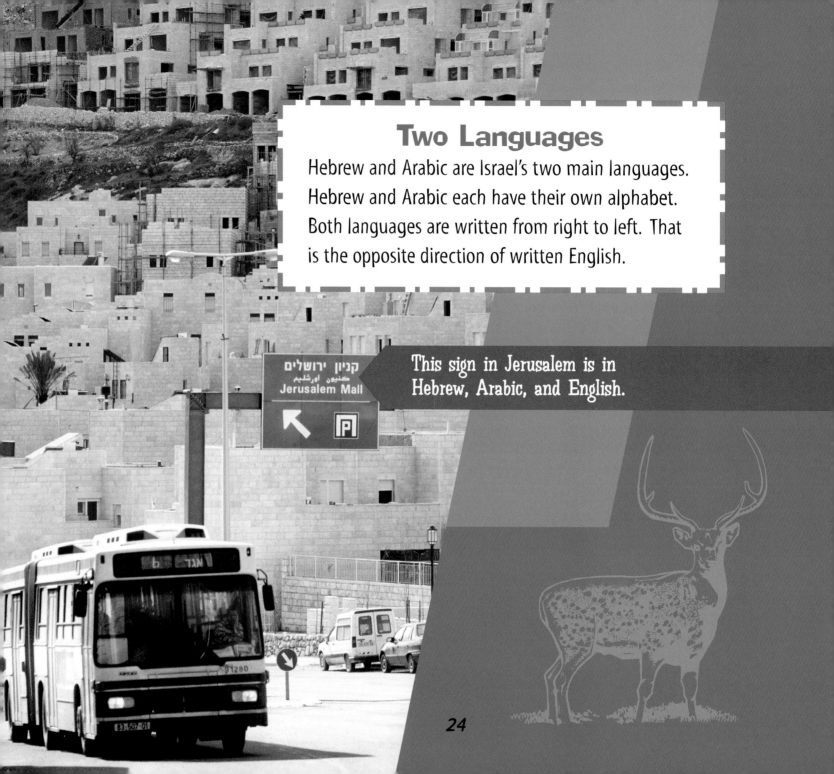

קניון ירושלים
كنيون اورشليم
Jerusalem Mall

This sign in Jerusalem is in Hebrew, Arabic, and English.

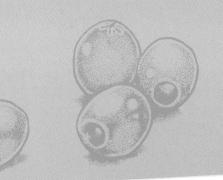

Eliezer Ben-Yehuda

In modern times, most Israelis speak Hebrew. But Hebrew has not always been the main language. For two thousand years, the Hebrew language was only used for prayers. Jewish people spoke many different languages.

In 1881, Eliezer Ben-Yehuda moved to Israel. He worked to make Hebrew the national language spoken by Jews in Israel. His work paid off in 1922. Hebrew became the official language of Jews in Israel.

Books in Israel are commonly printed in Hebrew.

Celebrate!

Jewish Israelis have many holidays. In the fall, they celebrate Rosh Hashana. That is the Jewish New Year. People celebrate by saying prayers. They have a special dinner with family and friends. Yom Kippur is another Jewish holiday. It is a time for Jews to fast. That means they do not eat or drink.

A blast from the shofar (a ram's-horn trumpet) signals the start of Rosh Hashana.

26

This little girl dressed up in a costume for a Purim parade in Jerusalem.

Purim!

Purim is a fun day for Jewish families. Purim is like Halloween and April Fool's Day in one. Newspapers run made-up stories. People have costume parties. Colorful parades wind through the streets.

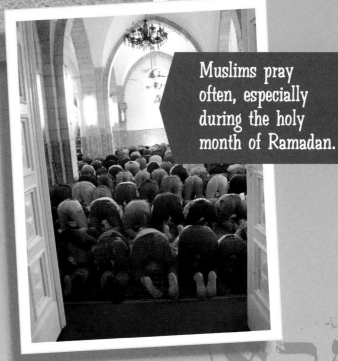

Muslims pray often, especially during the holy month of Ramadan.

Ramadan is an important Muslim holiday. Ramadan is the Muslim holy month. At that time, Muslims pray and worship often. They also fast from sunrise to sunset. Ramadan ends with Eid al-Fitr. Eid al-Fitr is a three-day party.

School Days

Kids in Israel go to school six days a week. Jewish kids get Saturdays off. Muslim kids have Fridays off. Those are the holy days in their religions.

These third-grade boys study at a Jewish school.

Jews and Muslims go to separate schools. Jewish students learn their lessons in Hebrew. Muslim students learn theirs in Arabic.

Plant a Tree!

Tu B'Shevat is a special day in Israel. On that day, schoolchildren plant trees (*above*). Over the years, kids have planted more than 200 million trees.

These Muslim girls are taught in Arabic.

Growing Up

Jewish kids have a special ceremony when they turn thirteen. Boys have a bar mitzvah. Girls have a bat mitzvah. The ceremonies celebrate Jewish boys and girls becoming adults. After the ceremony, families usually have a celebration.

Eighteen is also an important age for Israelis. At this age, Israeli teenagers must join the military service. Men serve for three years. Women serve for two years.

Young women train in the Israeli military.

This Jewish boy is blessed by his father during his bar mitzvah.

Snack Break

When you get hungry in Israel, you can choose from many tasty foods. Falafel is a favorite treat. Falafel is made of mashed, fried chickpeas. It is served in pita bread. Israelis top it off with salad and a special sauce.

Falafel is a popular street food in Israeli cities.

At the Market

Israelis can buy their food at the supermarket. But most Israelis shop at small corner stores. Others like to shop at *shuks*. Shuks are outdoor markets. Sellers and buyers bargain at shuks. That means they talk until they agree on a price.

Vegetable markets like this one are common in Israel.

Some Israelis stop for a burger and fries. Others choose delicious fresh fruit for a healthy snack. Israelis believe that they grow the world's best fruit. Oranges and dates are two yummy snacks.

Time to Play!

Many Israelis like to play sports. Soccer is the most popular game. Kids play in school yards or join youth leagues. Fans pack the stadiums to cheer for their favorite teams.

Adults watch these young boys play soccer in Israel.

A runner takes her mark at the Maccabiah Games.

Judah Maccabee

The Maccabiah Games are named for Judah Maccabee. He was an ancient Jewish warrior. He fought against the ancient Greeks.

Israel hosts its own Olympic-style games every four years. They're called the Maccabiah Games. Jewish athletes from around the world compete. They might play basketball, volleyball, field hockey, track and field, tennis, or water sports.

Art Everywhere

Art is easy to find in Israel. Beautiful stained glass windows decorate the Hadassah Hospital in Jerusalem. Colorful mosaics decorate Muslim mosques. Mosaics are pictures made with pieces of colored glass, stone, or tile.

This is one of the stained glass windows at Hadassah Hospital.

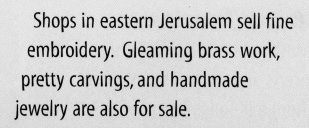

Shops in eastern Jerusalem sell fine embroidery. Gleaming brass work, pretty carvings, and handmade jewelry are also for sale.

Dig it!

Many Israelis want to learn about the country's past. Experts dig into hillsides to find the ruins of ancient cities. Studying the ruins helps them learn what life was like long ago.

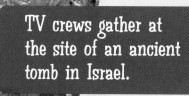

TV crews gather at the site of an ancient tomb in Israel.

Tunes and Twirls

Music is popular in Israel. Most cities and towns have an orchestra. Israelis go to concerts and nightclubs. Modern music sometimes borrows from folk songs and poetry.

Israeli girls take part in a traditional folk dance.

38

Many people enjoy klezmer music. Klezmer music has a lively beat. It makes people want to stomp their feet. Dancing is a fun way to spend an evening. The hora is the traditional folk dance of Israel. This is a whirling circle dance.

Klezmer music is popular in Israel.

Good Book!

Looking for something to read? Visit a bookstore. Most city streets have newsstands too. Newsstands are packed with newspapers and magazines. And they come in many different languages.

This woman reads a book at a secondhand bookstore in Jerusalem.

Hebrew Book Week takes place every year. Cities and towns turn their public squares and parks into large, outdoor bookstores. Israelis find enough good deals to fill their bookshelves!

These Israeli girls take time out to read at a school in Jerusalem.

Folktales

Israeli kids love to hear folktales. Folktales are stories passed on from ancestors. Family members brought stories with them from all over the world. Here is a story told by Jewish people with Eastern European roots.

A man lived with his wife and many children in a tiny, busy, crowded house. The man wanted some peace and quiet, so he asked a rabbi what to do. The rabbi said, "Bring your chickens into your house." The man was surprised, but he did what the rabbi advised. The chickens made the noise and crowding worse! When the man went back for more advice, the rabbi told him to bring a different animal inside every day. The man brought in goats, ducks, and a cow. Fur, feathers, people, and noise filled the house. After a week, the rabbi advised the man to take the honking, clucking, mooing animals outside. That night, the man and his family slept in peace. The next morning, the man looked around his tiny house and said, "What a peaceful place!"

THE FLAG OF ISRAEL

Israel's flag has a blue Star of David on a white background. The Star of David is a six-pointed star. It is a symbol of the people of Israel. The star is centered between two blue stripes. This design is based on a *tallit*. That's a Jewish prayer shawl. The shawl has blue stripes on a white background. The flag was officially adopted on October 28, 1948.

FAST FACTS

FULL COUNTRY NAME: The State of Israel

AREA: 8,000 square miles (21,000 square kilometers). That is about as big as the state of New Jersey.

MAIN LANDFORMS: the coastal plains, the Negev desert, the Great Rift Valley, the highlands Samarian Hills and Judean Hills, the mountains Meron and Tabor

MAJOR RIVER: Jordan

ANIMALS AND THEIR HABITATS: wild boars, gazelles, and jackals (highlands); foxes and wildcats (wooded areas); snakes and lizards (desert); ibex (mountains)

CAPITAL CITY: Jerusalem

OFFICIAL LANGUAGES: Hebrew and Arabic

POPULATION: about 7,150,000

GLOSSARY

Arabs: modern-day relatives of the people who settled Israel in the 600s C.E.

bargain: to talk between a buyer and seller about the cost of an item. Bargaining ends when both sides agree on a price.

concentration camps: places where people are imprisoned and often killed without any legal process

desert: a dry, sandy region

folktales: stories told by word of mouth from grandparent to parent to child. Many folktales have been written down in books.

Great Rift Valley: a low area of Earth's surface that stretches from Syria to Mozambique. The Dead Sea is part of the Great Rift Valley.

highlands: an area with hills or mountains

kibbutz: an Israeli farming settlement where people share work and belongings

Middle East: a part of southwestern Asia that meets North Africa

mountain: a part of Earth's surface that rises high into the sky

nomad: a person who moves from place to place, following seasonal sources of water and food

plains: a broad, flat area of land that has few trees

rabbi: a teacher of the Jewish law

synagogue: a Jewish house of worship

TO LEARN MORE

BOOKS

Bacon, Josephine. *Cooking the Israeli Way.* Minneapolis: Lerner Publications Company, 2002. Taste the flavors of Israel with the recipes in this book.

Greenfield, Howard. *A Promise Fulfilled: Theodor Herzl, Chaim Weizmann, David Ben-Gurion, and the Creation of the State of Israel.* New York: Greenwillow Books, 2005. This book describes how the state of Israel came to be.

Rouss, Sylvia A. *Sammy Spider's First Trip to Israel.* Minneapolis: Kar-Ben Publishing, 2002. Enjoy a fictional tale about a visit to Israel.

WEBSITES

Akhlah: Israel for Children
http://www.akhlah.com/israel/israel.php
See historical maps of Israel, read about the holidays Israelis celebrate, and even learn a little Hebrew.

Dolphin Reef's Home Page
http://www.dolphinreef.co.il
Learn about Dolphin Reef Eilat, on the shore of the Red Sea, where you can meet a whole family of dolphins.

Israel4Kids
http://israelemb.org/kids
Learn about the history of Israel, the symbols of the country, or tour famous places on this site run by the Israeli Embassy in the United States.

INDEX

The images in this book are used with the permission of: © Ilan Arad/Getty Images, p. 4; © Fred Bruemmer/Peter Arnold, Inc., pp. 6, 7; © Helene Rogers/ Art Directors, p. 8; © Adina Tovy/Art Directors, p. 9 (left); The State of Israel National Photo Collection, p. 9 (right); © Tom Stoddart Archive/Hulton Archive/ Getty Images, p. 10; © Greer & Associates, Inc./SuperStock, p. 11; Courtesy of the Israel Ministry of Tourism, p. 12; © Menahem Kahana/AFP/Getty Images, p. 13; © Rafael Ben-Ari/ZUMA Press, p. 14; © John R. Kreul/Independent Picture Service, pp. 15, 33; © Teun Voeten/Panos Pictures, pp. 16, 29 (left); © Gali Tibbon/AFP/Getty Images, p. 17; © Rafael Ben-Ari/Art Directors, p. 18; © Ahikam Seril/Panos Pictures, p. 19; © Richard Nowitz, p. 20; © Ricki Rosen/CORBIS, pp. 21, 28; © Jeff Greenberg/Art Directors, p. 22; © Saif Dahlah/Getty Images, p. 23; © Achim Pohl/Peter Arnold, Inc., p. 24; © David Silverman/Getty Images, pp. 25, 37, 41; © Jack Guez/Getty Images, p. 26; © Paula Bronstein/Getty Images, p. 27 (left); © Hrvoje Polan/Getty Images, p. 27 (right); Courtesy of the Israel Ministry of Tourism, p. 29 (right); Courtesy of the IDF Archive, p. 30; © Dan Porges/Peter Arnold, Inc., p. 31; © AA World Travel Library/Alamy, p. 32; © Israel Images/Alamy, pp. 32, 38; ©Alan Gignoux/Alamy, p. 34; Maccabiah USA/Sports for Israel, p. 35; ©SuperStock, Inc./ SuperStock, p. 36; © Yoel Harel/Alamy, p. 39 (right); © Lebrecht Music and Arts Photo Library/Alamy, p. 39 (left); © Eddie Gerald/Alamy, p. 40, Illustrations by © Bill Hauser/Independent Picture Service.

Cover: © age fotostock/SuperStock.